Fashion Design Illustration

Women

Fashion Design Illustration

Women

Patrick John Ireland

B. T. BATSFORD LTD · LONDON

Typeset by Servis Filmsetting Ltd, Manchester

and printed in Great Britain by
The Bath Press, Bath

for the publishers
B. T. Batsford Ltd
4 Fitzhardinge Street
London W1H 0AH

ISBN 0 7134 6622 7

A CIP catalogue record for this book is available from the British Library

Acknowledgements

I would like to extend my thanks to the Bournemouth College of Art and Design, the Cordwainer's College, London and all the students and lecturers in the many colleges and workshops I have worked with for their encouragement in producing this book.

Thanks also to Ann Ward for her helpful advice, Richard Reynolds and Kate Bell, my editors at B. T. Batsford, and finally to Sue Lacey who designed the book.

Photographs by Rainer Usselmann.

CONTENTS

The purpose of this book is to help design students to develop fashion sketching techniques and the skills of creating and communicating design ideas. The designer should possess a general awareness of fashion and a sound knowledge of fabrics and the use of colour. He or she should be capable of finding inspiration from many different sources, and should be able to develop these ideas to create original designs. A sound knowledge of both pattern-cutting and the methods of making up garments are also necessary requirements.

Initially, many students of design find it difficult to express their ideas on paper and need help in acquiring good fashion drawing techniques. This book is arranged in sections to cover the different stages in the fashion process. It shows how the fashion figure can be developed, working from the basic proportions of the figure, by creating and utilizing figure templates. In the early stages, the beginner can copy or trace figure templates directly from this book, over which design ideas may be developed with the aid of semi-transparent paper or a light box. The fashion designer needs to develop a style of drawing that is clear, fluent and adaptable. Costume and life classes are extremely helpful, and should be attended if at all possible. The different methods illustrated in this book should help the student to produce attractive and functional fashion design drawings.

There are three stages of drawing when designing:

1 Design development

In the earliest stages of developing a design, the designer's sketches should be fairly rough, exploring and experimenting with the many possibilities within each idea or theme. These groups of drawings are known at this stage as design development sheets. They should indicate design ideas, illustrating both the front and back views of the garments illustrated. The types of fabric, pattern and texture should also be suggested, perhaps with a sample fabric attached to the sheet. Notes can be added to convey any details not shown in the sketch.

2 Production drawings

When a design has been approved, a sample garment will be requested. The production team will need a specification sheet and a production drawing of the design for this purpose. This drawing has to be clear and diagrammatic in order to show details of the cut, seam and dart placement and any proposed style features.

3 Presentation drawings

Presentation drawings are used to present a collection of design ideas to a client. They should be finished drawings which project the intended fashion image of the designs. This means that careful thought should be given, not only to the drawing of the garments, but also to the pose of the figures, hairstyles and accessories, in order to achieve an attractive overall effect. Different ways of presenting the work should also be developed, taking into account the colours and patterns of the fabrics. The designer should become adept at using colour in presentation drawings, to suggest the effects of pattern and texture. The colours of the fabrics chosen for a design should always be accurately represented in presentation drawings.

Layout and presentation effects

Presentation drawings are used on many different

occasions: when showing design ideas to clients, entering competitions, setting up displays, as well as for portfolio work for interviews and assessments.

Many different techniques may be used for the presentation of work. The layout and mounting, especially, need to be carefully considered. Photographs, sketches and decorative effects can be introduced, often as a backdrop, to complement the design drawing. The photocopier can also be a valuable tool. However, you should take care never to let the presentation of your work overpower the design drawing itself. Examples of different presentation drawings are given in the later sections of the book.

Fashion illustration

The fashion illustrator works in a specialized area of advertising and marketing, producing drawings for promotional magazines and newspapers, as well as publicity material for catalogues and stores. Fashion drawings are also used for window displays and exhibition stands. A further area of work is the production of fashion prediction trend drawings.

Fashion illustrators are often trained as graphic designers. However, many illustrators start fashion drawing while studying on fashion design courses. Styles of drawing vary considerably. Glossy magazines and stores with a high fashion image tend to use elegant and freestyle kinds of drawings. Drawing styles are constantly changing to reflect the influences and moods of fashion at any particular time.

Drawing the Figure

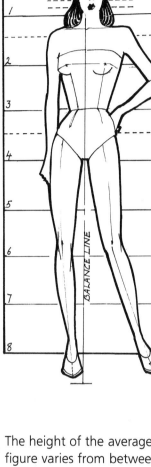

The height of the average figure varies from between seven-and-a-half to eight times the height of the head. When drawing a fashion sketch, the proportions are usually eight to eight-and-a-half with exaggeration on the length of the legs. Try not to over-exaggerate when producing sketches, however, as this may distort the proportions of your design.

When sketching, draw the figure first with very light pencil lines and check that the positions of the bust, waist and hips are correct, as well as the overall proportions. When sketching, you will find it helpful to draw a faint line following the contour centre of the body (see page 8). The vertical balance line should be drawn from the pit of the neck to the foot that is carrying the weight of the body, to indicate that the head and neck are aligned with the supporting foot. This will serve as a guide when designing and positioning relative details.

Basic figure drawing

In order to express your design ideas precisely, and to present them attractively, you will need to develop your skills in figure drawing. When designing, you should be able to sketch a figure from memory in a number of different poses.

Start by studying figure drawing, until you can memorize the correct proportions and draw freehand figures with confidence.

I have grouped the different techniques of drawing the fashion figure under the following headings:

1 Drawing the figure – basic proportion
2 Drawing from templates
3 Drawing from the imagination – stylized drawings
4 Drawing from photographs
5 Drawing from life

Even if you are unable to attend life-drawing and costume classes, you will find the methods illustrated in this book a valuable aid to developing your figure drawing techniques.

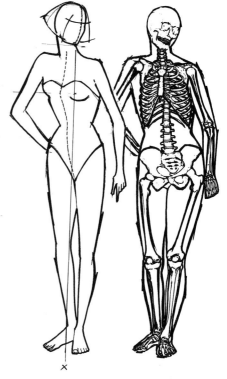

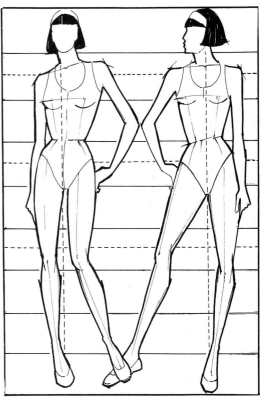

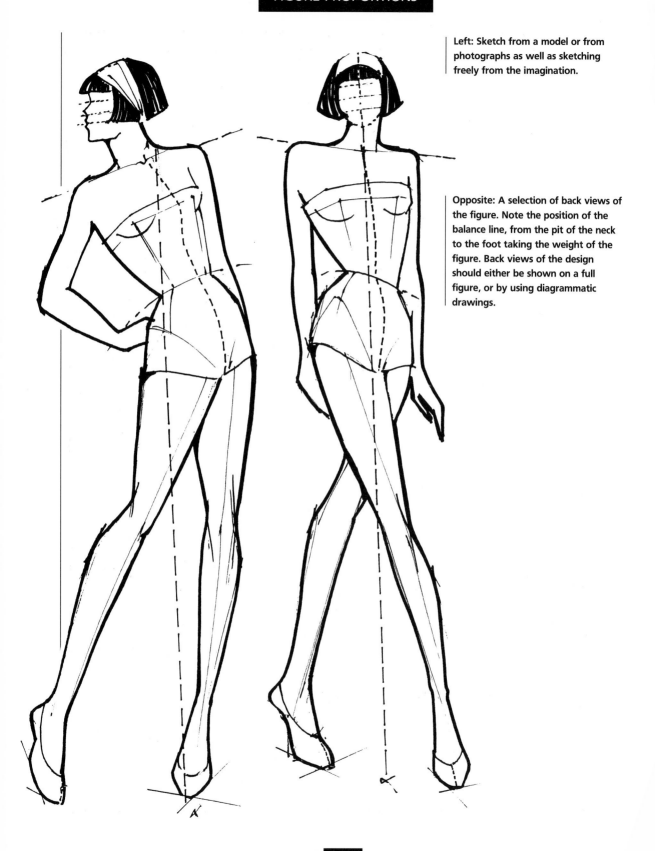

Left: Sketch from a model or from photographs as well as sketching freely from the imagination.

Opposite: A selection of back views of the figure. Note the position of the balance line, from the pit of the neck to the foot taking the weight of the figure. Back views of the design should either be shown on a full figure, or by using diagrammatic drawings.

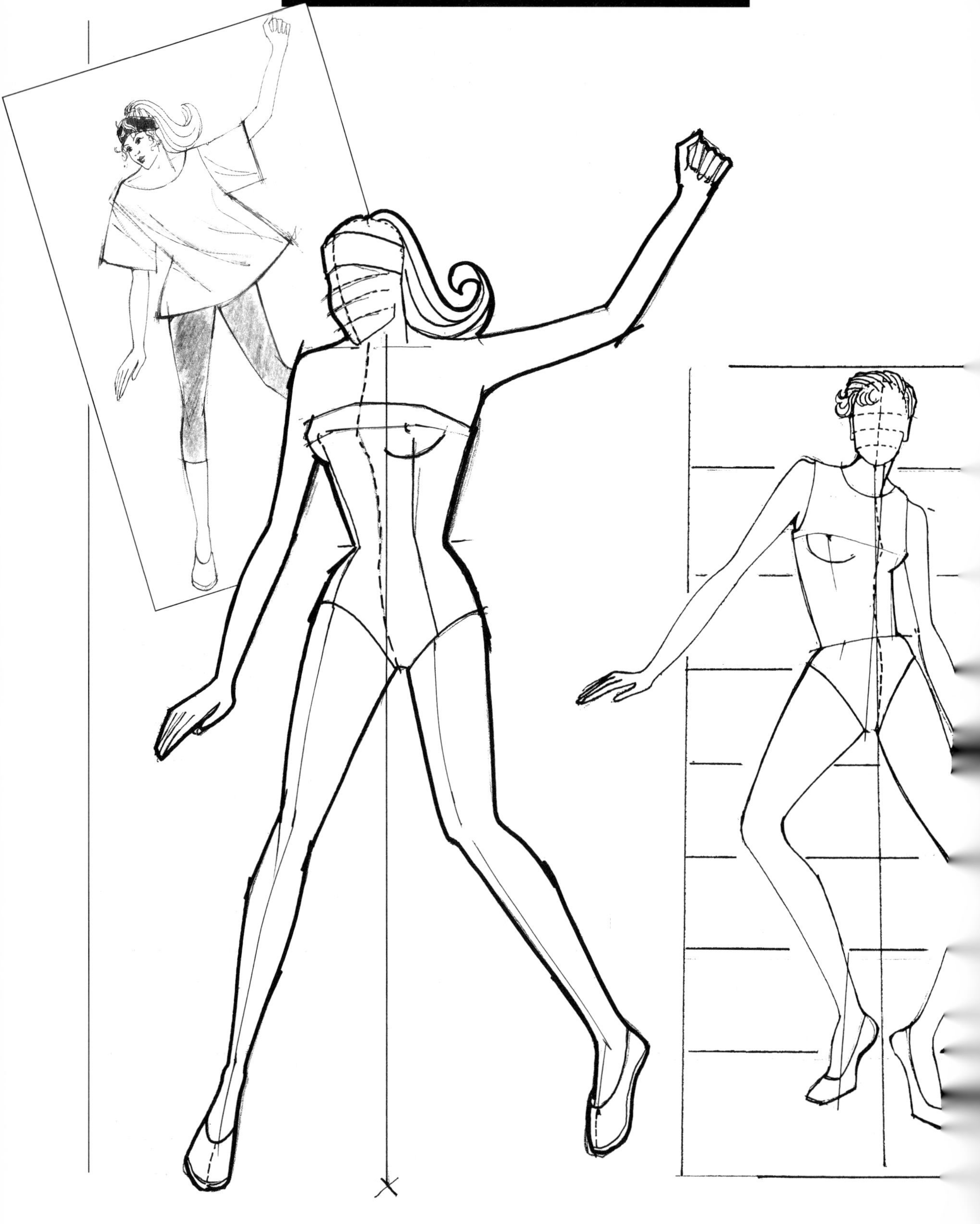

When design sketching, the mood of the design can be effectively evoked by sketching a pose which reflects some kind of relevant activity, i.e. dancing, athletics, etc.

Different methods may be used to achieve the required effect. Work from a model, photographs, or develop a pose from your imagination using the grid. Students in the early stages can try working from the templates illustrated in this book.

Opposite: Sketch developed over the template. Note the balance line from the pit of the neck to the floor, indicating how the weight of the body is supported evenly on both feet. The swing of the hair and movement of the T-shirt contribute to the general mood of the drawing.

A selection of figures in active poses. Note the centre front line and balance line.

A selection of fashion sketches which have been developed over the templates illustrated here, using both semi-transparent layout paper and a light box. The figures have been adapted by the introduction of different hairstyles and features.

Develop templates of your own, working from photographs. Designs can be developed by working over the figures, using layout paper.

For practice in designing over a template, you may either trace the figure poses from this section, or preferably, construct your own figures using the methods illustrated, working from the grid.

The technique of drawing garments over a figure guide can be used to develop your own design ideas. By drawing a series of simple figures, including both front and back views as illustrated here, you can go on to create a variety of different designs for a garment. The resulting collection of drawings may be used as a design sheet.

Work around the outline of the figure to create your own design, remembering to take into account the type of fabric you have selected, and the way in which the material will gather and fall.

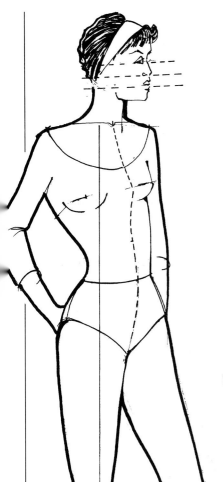

Creating and using templates

1 Sketch the figure.

2 Place layout paper over the figure template. The outline of the figure should be clearly visible through the semi-transparent paper.

3 Develop the design sketch, remembering to relate the details to the overall proportions of the figure. The balance line falls from the pit of the neck to the foot, taking the weight of the body. Develop the pose by altering the angle of the hips and shoulders.

Sketches produced over templates using a soft black pencil for shading and a Fine Artline pen for the details. Note how the shading on one side of the figure is made darker to give extra dimension to the sketch.

You should keep your figure basic to start with, confining the depiction of the face, hair, hands and feet to the simplest of indications, until you have had more time to practise and gain confidence. Later on, as you become more experienced in figure drawing, you will be able to develop different poses using this method.

Notice the fullness of the folds and gathers that can be achieved by careful shading.

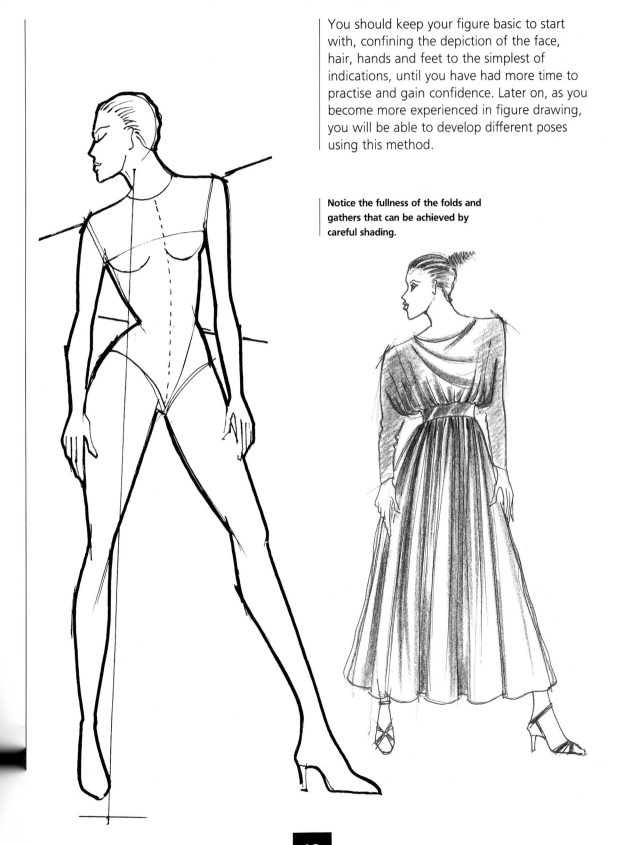

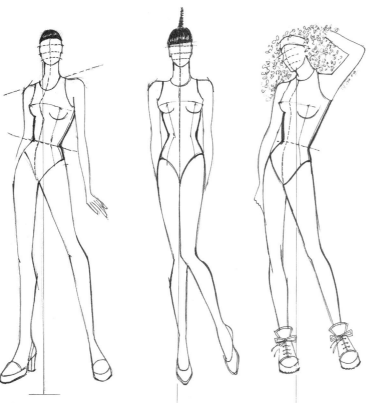

The drawings illustrated are highly stylized to project a particular fashion image, using exaggerated poses and proportions. Certain features of the garments have been highlighted for particular emphasis. If the garments in this drawing were to be made up in the sample room, working drawings to the normal scale would be included.

Stylized drawings

Stylized drawings are often extreme and exaggerated in their proportions, to give emphasis to the fashion image. The sketches should have a sense of fun and style. In a stylized drawing, certain features of the garments are singled out. This may be done by drawing very exaggerated legs to highlight a short skirt, or by sketching a very full sleeve or an outsize collar to dramatize these features.

Stylized drawings are often used by fashion students when developing design ideas and producing presentation work, as they can be used to project a very strong image. The technique is therefore particularly effective when drawing futuristic or avante-garde fashions. Working drawings showing the true proportions of the garments should always be shown alongside a stylized design drawing.

In this drawing, the length of the legs and the small size of the head have been exaggerated to give emphasis to the fashion image. Note the use of two thicknesses of black pen. A cool grey Magic Marker pen has been used for tonal effect. The fur trim has been suggested using a Pilot Hi-Tecpoint V5 extra fine pen.

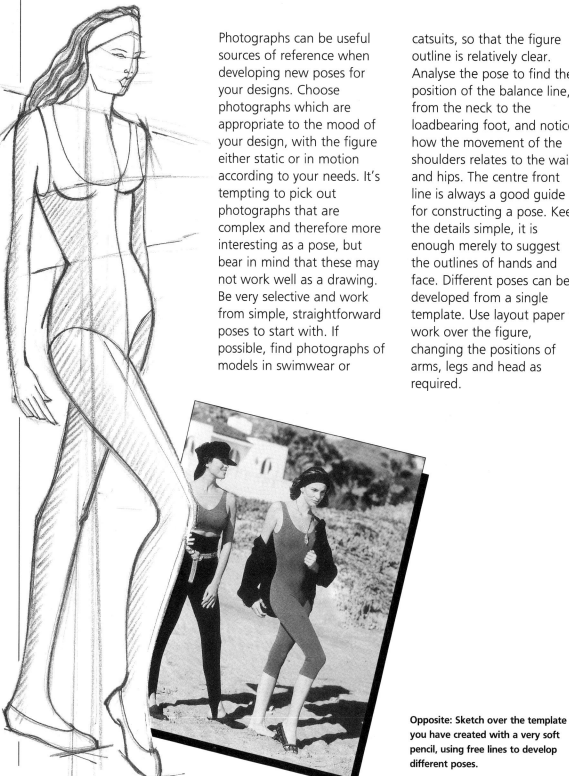

Photographs can be useful sources of reference when developing new poses for your designs. Choose photographs which are appropriate to the mood of your design, with the figure either static or in motion according to your needs. It's tempting to pick out photographs that are complex and therefore more interesting as a pose, but bear in mind that these may not work well as a drawing. Be very selective and work from simple, straightforward poses to start with. If possible, find photographs of models in swimwear or catsuits, so that the figure outline is relatively clear. Analyse the pose to find the position of the balance line, from the neck to the loadbearing foot, and notice how the movement of the shoulders relates to the waist and hips. The centre front line is always a good guide for constructing a pose. Keep the details simple, it is enough merely to suggest the outlines of hands and face. Different poses can be developed from a single template. Use layout paper to work over the figure, changing the positions of arms, legs and head as required.

Opposite: Sketch over the template you have created with a very soft pencil, using free lines to develop different poses.

Most fashion design courses have special periods allotted to life and fashion drawing. The length of the different poses will vary from between five and twenty minutes. Ask a friend to model for you to give you extra practise in drawing from life.

Practise creating new poses by working from the life model, and study the way in which the folds and gathers of a garment alter as the model moves. Experiment using different media and various grades of paper, and try making both large and small drawings,

working with both very free and more controlled techniques.

As a useful exercise, try sketching quick poses of two to five minutes, working using a very free line technique. Add tone with a watercolour wash or a pale grey marker pen. This kind of sketch may be developed later, and used as a template for further designs.

1   Start by working with a soft pencil, using a few lines to give the general outline of the movement of the pose.

2   Develop the drawing using a black Schwan Stabilo Softcolour pencil, using different amounts of pressure when shading. Note the dark to light effect obtained by shading from the left side of the figure to the right.

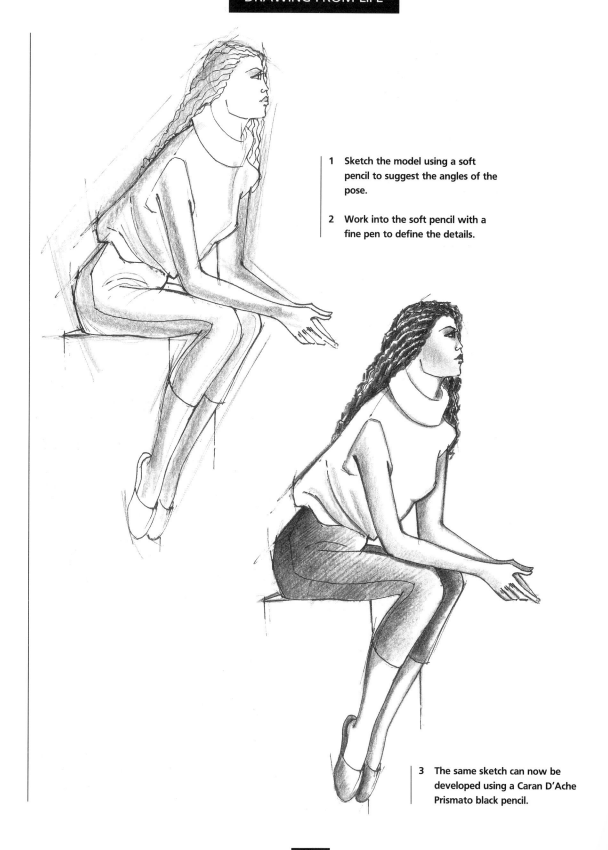

1   Sketch the model using a soft
    pencil to suggest the angles of the
    pose.

2   Work into the soft pencil with a
    fine pen to define the details.

3   The same sketch can now be
    developed using a Caran D'Ache
    Prismato black pencil.

1 Pen drawing produced using a Fine Artline 200 04 pen. A soft grey lead pencil was used to add tone values.

2 The same sketch developed with a different technique, using a Schwan Stabilo soft black pastel pencil.

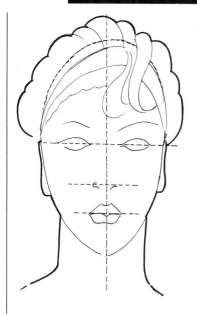

A simple method of drawing the head. Note the positioning of the features and guideline indicating the balance and proportions.

The drawing of the face and hair plays a major role in reflecting the fashion image that you wish to project in your design.

The face may be merely suggested, using a few lines, or worked up in greater detail. The style may be very realistic, or more stylized.

Fashions in hairstyles vary from a simple, clear-cut outline, to a more elaborate style, which might be dressed with flowers, clips or headbands.

Observe new trends, and note the many different techniques of make-up application and colouring.

The emphasis may be on the eyes, with focus on the eyelids and the shaping of the eyebrows, or on the lips and cheekbones.

Keep a sketchbook of current looks, collect cuttings from magazines and make a note of the different styles when attending fashion shows.

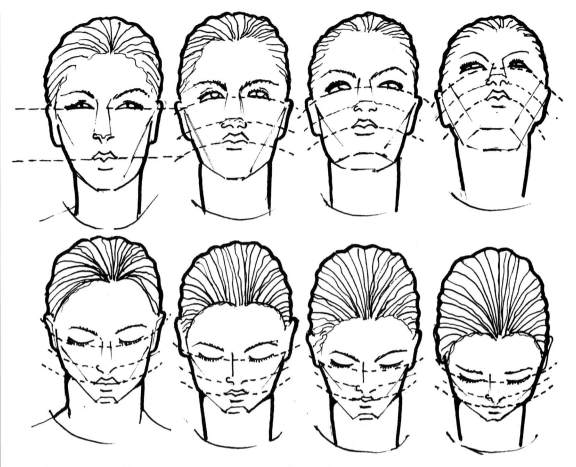

Drawing the head from different angles. Note the construction lines used to produce the correct perspective.

Practise sketching the head from different positions working from a model.

The drawing of the face and hair plays a major role in reflecting the fashion image that you wish to project in your design. The face may be merely suggested, using a few lines, or worked up in greater detail. The style may be very realistic, or more stylized.

Fashions in hairstyles vary from a simple, clear-cut outline, to a more elaborate style, which might be dressed with flowers, clips or headbands.

Observe new trends, and note the many different techniques of make-up application and colouring. The emphasis may be on the eyes, with focus on the eyelids and the shaping of the eyebrows, or on the lips and cheekbones.

Keep a sketchbook of current looks, collect cuttings from magazines and make a note of the different styles when attending fashion shows.

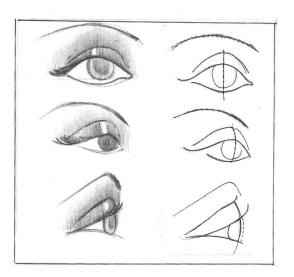

In fashion drawings, the facial features are often only suggested with the simplest of lines. In order to execute this successfully, make a study of the features from a life model, drawing the nose and eyes from many different angles.

Fashions in make-up and hairstyles often reflect former eras such as the Hollywood glamour years, the forties, fifties or sixties. Use your sketchbook to experiment with different techniques of portraying hairstyles and facial features – lips, eyes and nose. It is important to practise sketching the head from different angles, including back, side and three-quarter views.

Practise sketching faces from life, from photographs and from the imagination. Note the variety in facial shape and features, and again, draw from all angles.

A selection of different styles developed from the basic shape of the head. This is a good way of working when developing and experimenting with new ideas. Keep the sketch basic, either omitting the features of the face, or indicating them with a few simple lines, as illustrated here.

When designing hats, it is very important to develop your design ideas on a theme. The design sketches are the starting point before the designs are developed further in the workroom, using a selection of different materials modelled on the milliner's block. Design ideas can be worked up using felt hoods, straw, leather and draped fabrics. Variations can be achieved by using trimmings such as braids, flowers, feathers, nets and so on.

When drawing hats, make sure the hat is correctly placed on the head. Draw the shape of the head with light pencil lines, and then sketch your designs over this outline, making sure that the hat is in the correct position.

Practise sketching different styles from a milliner's block, working from various angles. Remember to take into account the way in which the hat will appear from the side and back views as well as from the front.

Arrange for a friend to model a hat for you. This will help when you come to design and sketch your own ideas from your imagination.

The hats illustrated here have been constructed around the basic shape of the head, with the facial features added in to complement the designs. The style of drawing shown here would be suitable for presenting a collection of drawings to a client. When developing your ideas, it is not always necessary to sketch facial features and hairstyles in great detail.

Note the construction lines of the head and features shown here. Again, this style of drawing would be suitable for presenting and showing a collection. The effects have been achieved using a soft black Rexel Cumberland pencil.

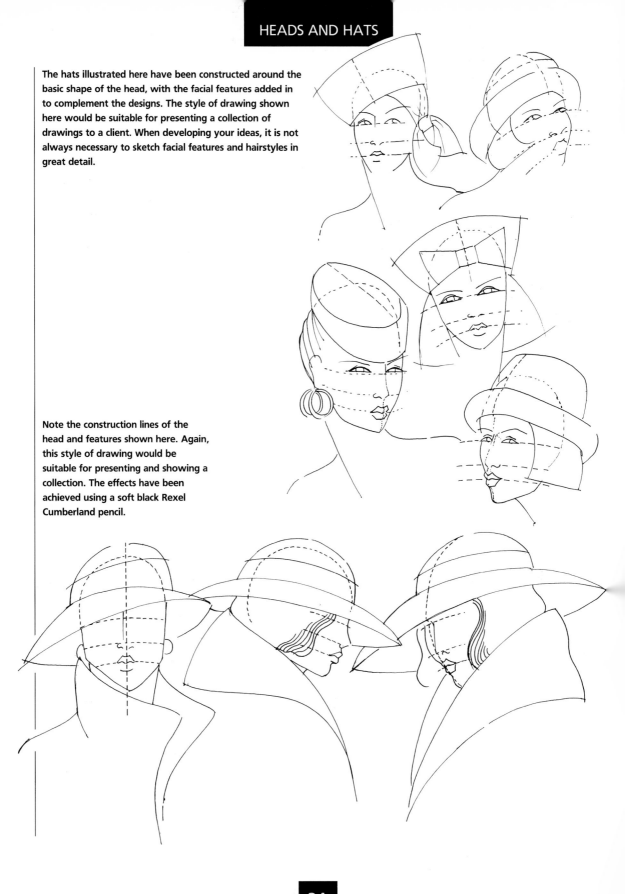

Balance the hat from the centre front line, taking into account the angle of the hat in relation to the face and hairstyle. Design the shape of the hat around the head, remembering to consider the back view by imagining that the head is transparent.

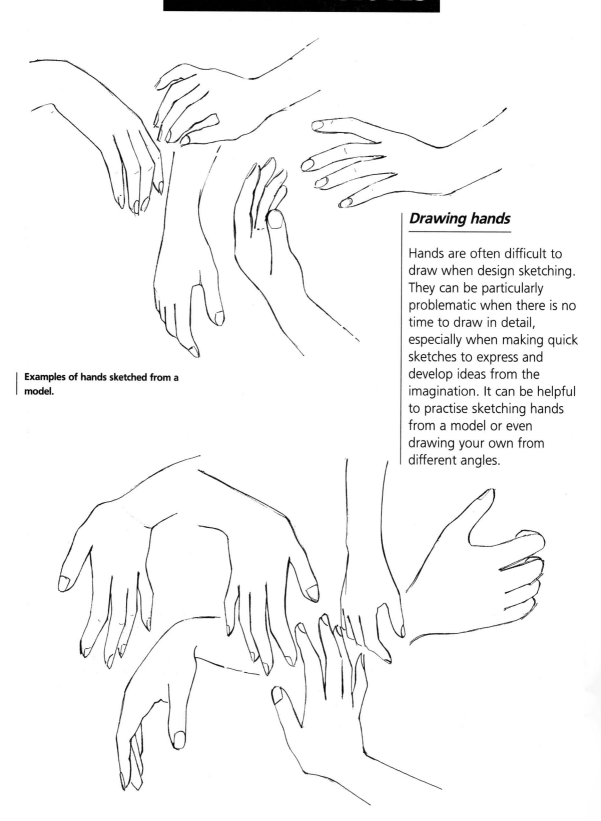

Examples of hands sketched from a model.

Drawing hands

Hands are often difficult to draw when design sketching. They can be particularly problematic when there is no time to draw in detail, especially when making quick sketches to express and develop ideas from the imagination. It can be helpful to practise sketching hands from a model or even drawing your own from different angles.

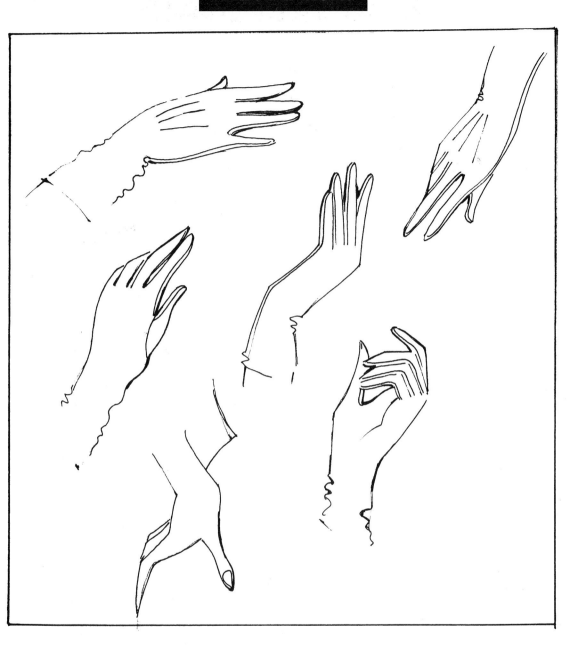

Use your sketches to construct a series of simple hand positions, but reworking or tracing over the original drawings. Use as few lines as possible to gain the required effect. A simple indication of the outline can look more effective than drawing the hands in detail.

Practise drawing hands in gloves from life. Note how the seams have been indicated on the fingers on these drawings.

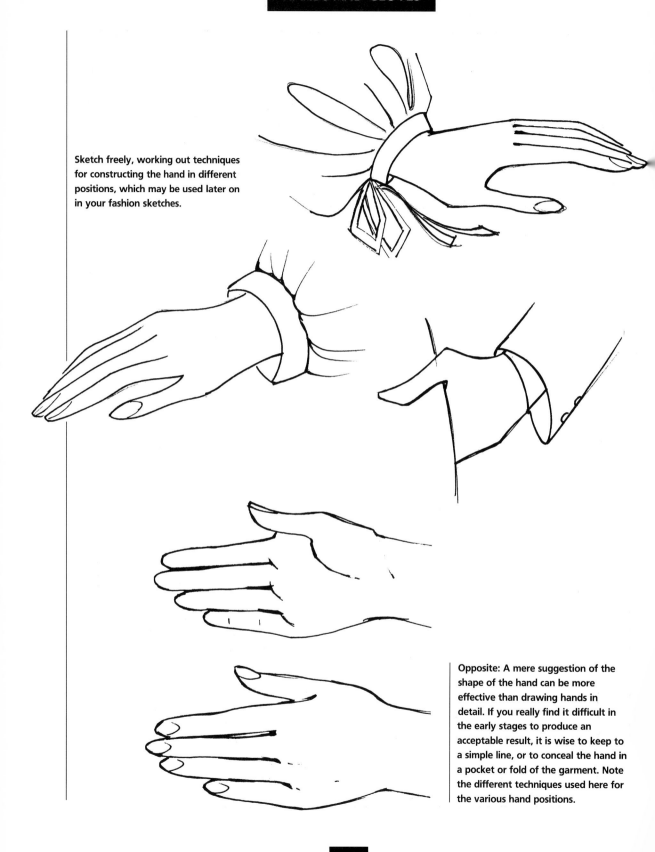

Sketch freely, working out techniques for constructing the hand in different positions, which may be used later on in your fashion sketches.

Opposite: A mere suggestion of the shape of the hand can be more effective than drawing hands in detail. If you really find it difficult in the early stages to produce an acceptable result, it is wise to keep to a simple line, or to conceal the hand in a pocket or fold of the garment. Note the different techniques used here for the various hand positions.

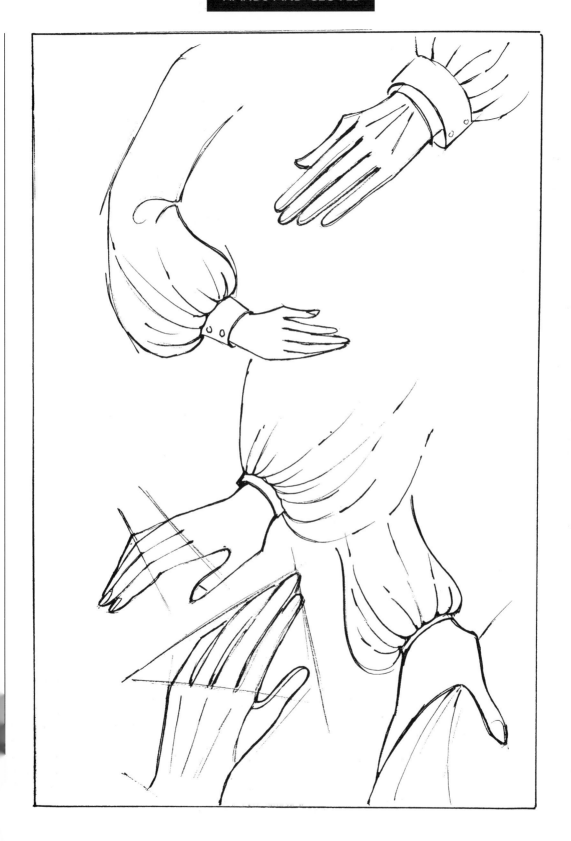

Drawing feet

Practise sketching legs and feet, either from a model or from photographs in fashion magazines. Lightly sketch the shape of the foot to indicate its position, using the method illustrated here. Keep a sketchbook of drawings, making a study of the foot. When you start sketching different shoe styles, it is always helpful to draw in the shape of the foot first with a light outline.

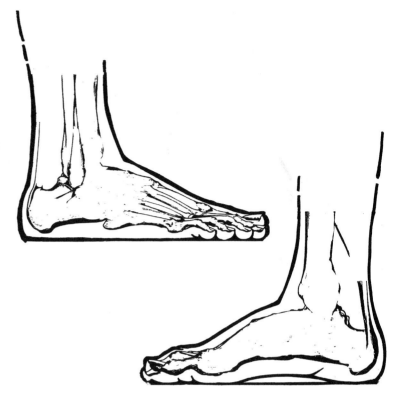

Some examples of feet drawn from life at different angles. Practise as much as you can to develop a natural line and flow in your drawings.

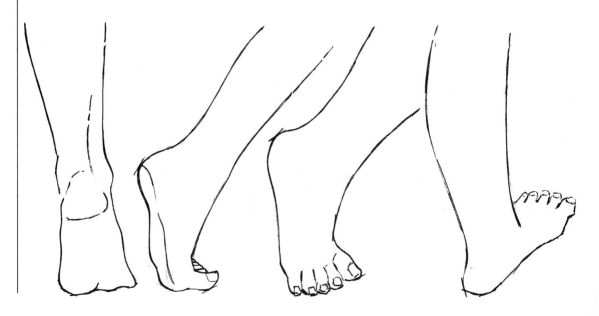

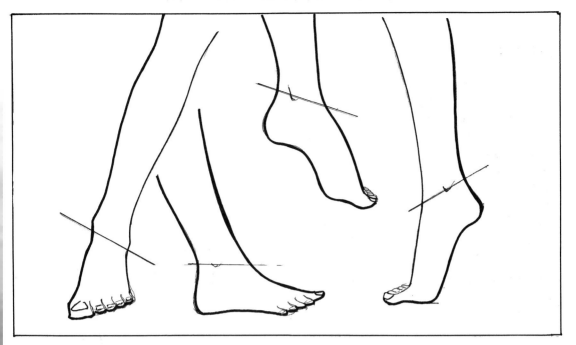

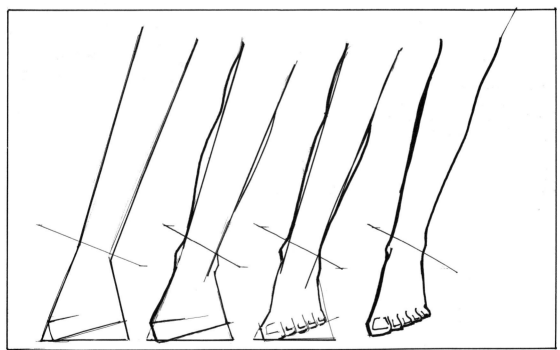

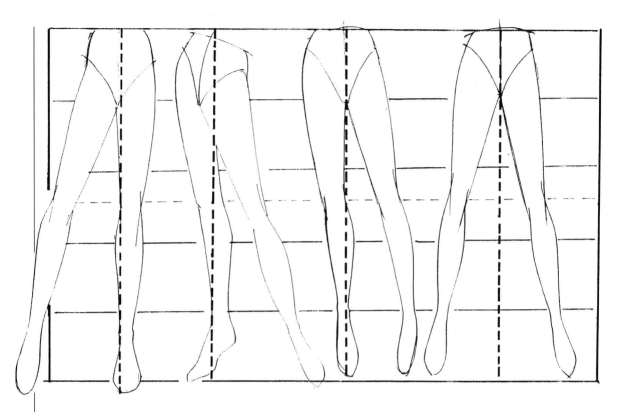

Practise drawing legs from the waist down, using the grid method and balance line to indicate which leg is taking the weight of the body.

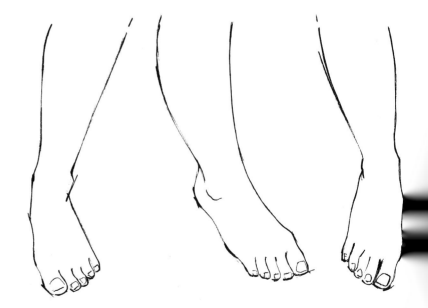

Experiment drawing feet from life, noting how the perspective alters with each change of position.

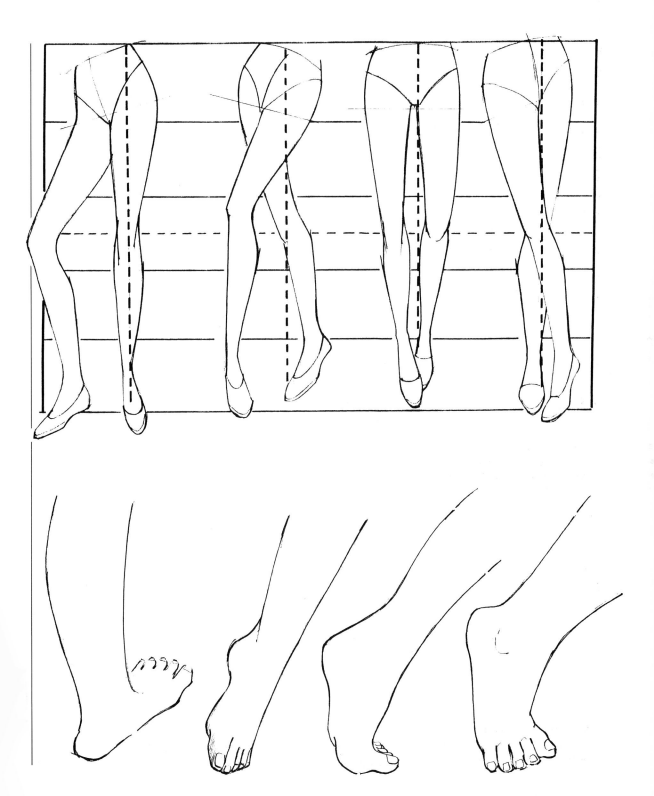

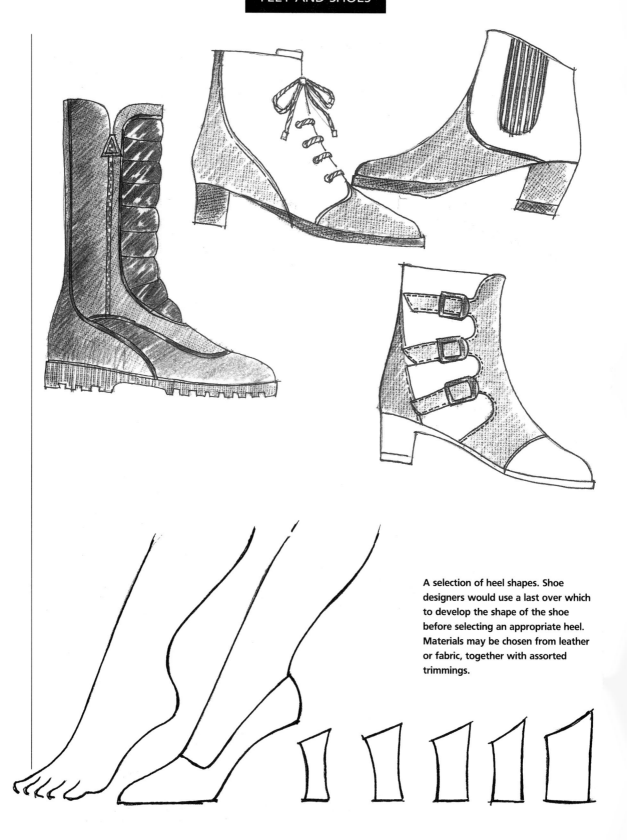

A selection of heel shapes. Shoe designers would use a last over which to develop the shape of the shoe before selecting an appropriate heel. Materials may be chosen from leather or fabric, together with assorted trimmings.

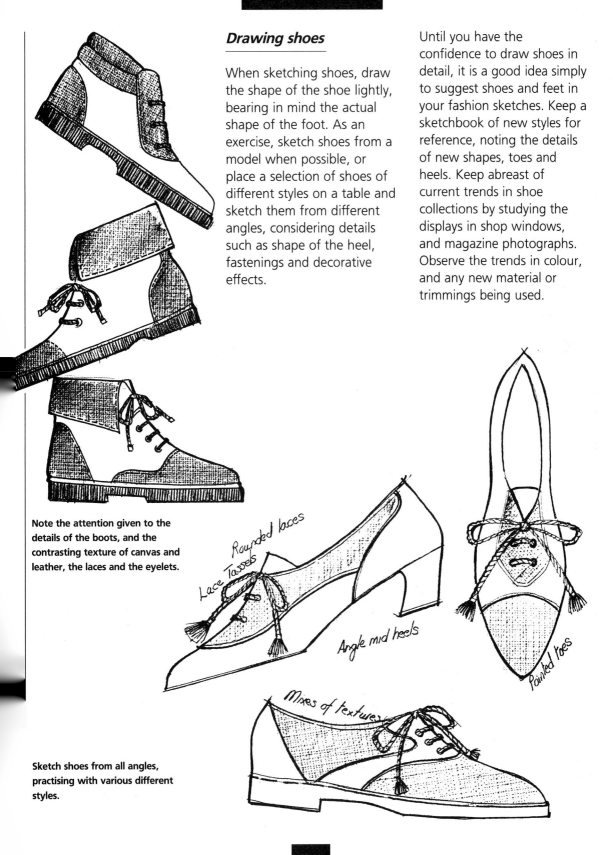

Drawing shoes

When sketching shoes, draw the shape of the shoe lightly, bearing in mind the actual shape of the foot. As an exercise, sketch shoes from a model when possible, or place a selection of shoes of different styles on a table and sketch them from different angles, considering details such as shape of the heel, fastenings and decorative effects.

Until you have the confidence to draw shoes in detail, it is a good idea simply to suggest shoes and feet in your fashion sketches. Keep a sketchbook of new styles for reference, noting the details of new shapes, toes and heels. Keep abreast of current trends in shoe collections by studying the displays in shop windows, and magazine photographs. Observe the trends in colour, and any new material or trimmings being used.

Note the attention given to the details of the boots, and the contrasting texture of canvas and leather, the laces and the eyelets.

Sketch shoes from all angles, practising with various different styles.

Rounded laces

Lace Tassels

Angle mid heels

Painted toes

Mixes of textures

As a useful exercise, sketch a selection of different styles. Always remember to work from the centre front line, drawing from front, back and side views.

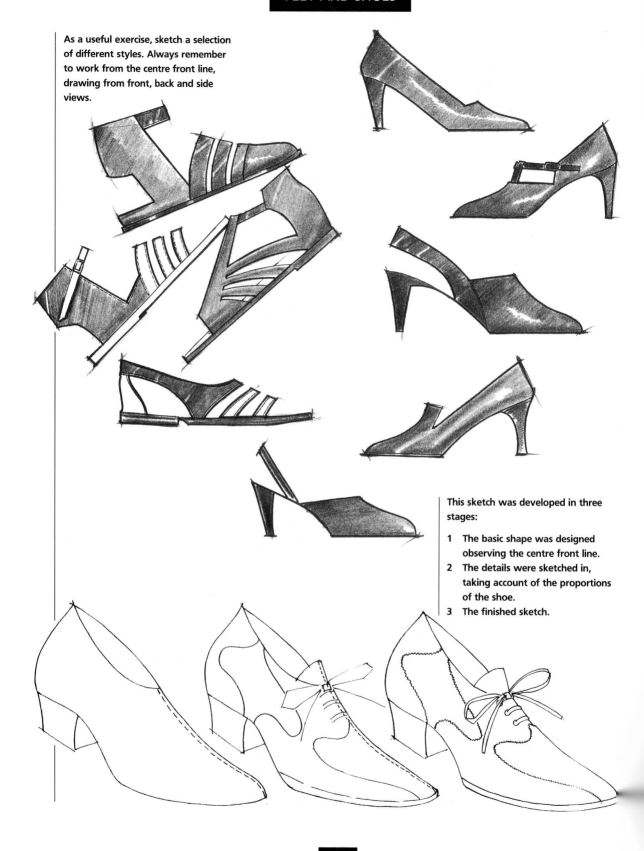

This sketch was developed in three stages:

1 The basic shape was designed observing the centre front line.
2 The details were sketched in, taking account of the proportions of the shoe.
3 The finished sketch.

A boot developed
in two stages.

Boots developed from a basic
template.

Drawing Details

When drawing frills on skirts, sleeves and hemlines, consider what fabric is being used and the way in which it will behave when gathered. Often the hemline will be uneven. Sketch in a light pencil line as a guide, to ensure that the hemline is balanced (indicated on these pages by a dotted line).

Design a collection incorporating frills and gathers. The use of a light watercolour wash, pale grey marker pen or a grey pencil can be very effective.

Note the use of a dotted line to ensure that the hemline is properly balanced.

Note how a few simple lines will suggest the frills without too much detail being required.

Create a collection of sketches of many different kinds of pleat, observing current trends and styles. Note how the various weights and textures of different fabrics affect the way in which the pleating falls.

These drawings show the use of different kinds of pleats, with a close-up detail of each. From left to right: knife, box, inverted, godet.

Examples of different kinds of pleats incorporated in short skirts. From left to right: panel, bias-cut, box, gathered.

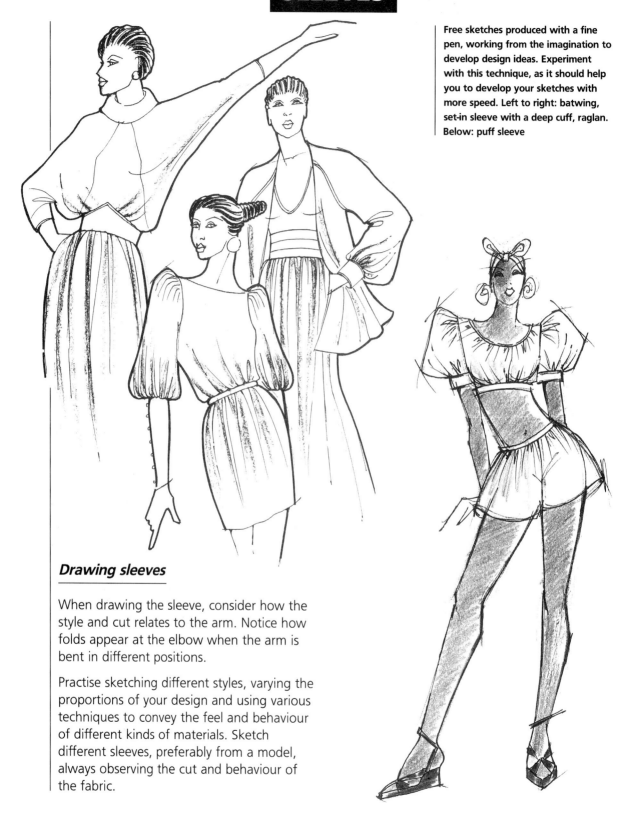

Free sketches produced with a fine pen, working from the imagination to develop design ideas. Experiment with this technique, as it should help you to develop your sketches with more speed. Left to right: batwing, set-in sleeve with a deep cuff, raglan. Below: puff sleeve

Drawing sleeves

When drawing the sleeve, consider how the style and cut relates to the arm. Notice how folds appear at the elbow when the arm is bent in different positions.

Practise sketching different styles, varying the proportions of your design and using various techniques to convey the feel and behaviour of different kinds of materials. Sketch different sleeves, preferably from a model, always observing the cut and behaviour of the fabric.

Kimono sleeve

Left to right: saddle, set-in shirt
sleeve.

Study the behaviour of different fabrics. Look at the way in which they drape, gather, pleat and fall into folds.

Arrange lengths of fabric on a dress stand and make sketches of the folds and drapes. Observe the qualities which characterize different materials.

Fabrics are an important source of inspiration for the designer. When design sketching, it is essential to suggest textures, patterns and the behaviour of different fabrics. Heavy fabrics, such as velvet or tweed, will produce completely different kinds of folds and gathers to light or transparent ones, such as chiffon.

Note the dotted line used to indicate the hem of the skirt and observe the way in which the fabric hangs and falls around the figure.

Drawing produced in two stages showing how folds can be defined using careful shading with a soft black pencil.

Full skirts illustrating deep folds. When adding colour or tone, remember that dark shading is used to indicate the depth of the fold. The deeper the fold, the darker the tone.

To construct this presentation drawing, the figure was first sketched, using a Fine Artline pen, and then coloured with a Letraset Pantone marker pen. The drawing was cut out and set against a simple panel to help the figure to stand out. Working drawings and sample fabrics were then arranged on the drawing to complement the presentation.

AUTUMN WINTER

Note the dotted line indicating the balance.

Single breasted

Double breasted

A selection of collar styles sketched from different angles.

Drawing Garments: Presentation Techniques

The following section demonstrates how to sketch designs for different occasions, employing a variety of presentation techniques. The poses have been selected to reflect the mood of the garments and the activities for which they have been designed.

Note the two stages of this sketch, which has been developed by using a template of a pose, especially chosen to complement the mood of the clothes. The drawing was produced using a black Fine Artline pen 04, and coloured with Softcolour Schwan Stabilo pencils. The folds of the trousers have been indicated with white paint.

Pens of different line values have been used in these drawings (black Fine Artline pen 04 and black Pentel Sign pen). Magic Marker pens were used for the patterns on the jacket and trousers. The poses were developed from magazine photographs.

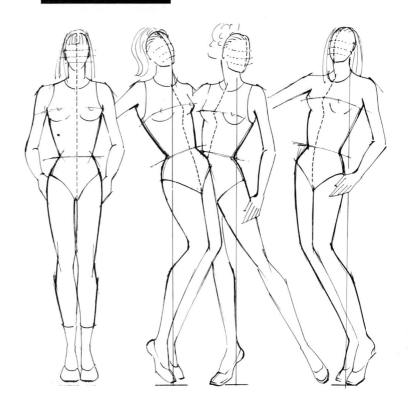

Different drawing techniques and media have been suggested, showing how illustrations can be developed in stages. Many ideas and examples have been given on the following pages of different ways in which design work may be presented.

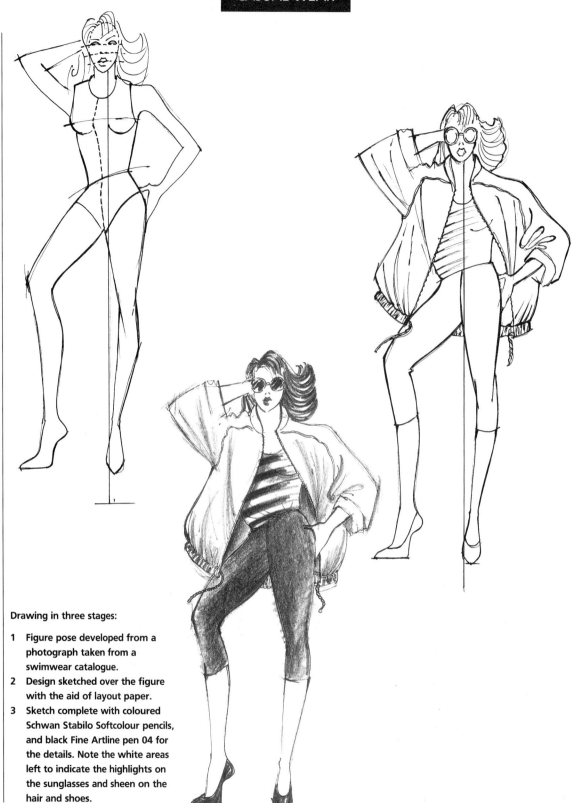

Drawing in three stages:

1 Figure pose developed from a photograph taken from a swimwear catalogue.
2 Design sketched over the figure with the aid of layout paper.
3 Sketch complete with coloured Schwan Stabilo Softcolour pencils, and black Fine Artline pen 04 for the details. Note the white areas left to indicate the highlights on the sunglasses and sheen on the hair and shoes.

This drawing was also completed in several stages:

1 The template was developed from a photograph.
2 The sketch was completed using a variety of line values and a bold black outline around the figure.
3 A patterned fabric was added to the finished drawing. To create this effect, the actual fabric was first photocopied and reduced to the scale of the drawing. The required shape was outlined against the sketch, cut out, and applied to the finished drawing.

Walking

1   A figure pose was drawn from the imagination using the grid method (illustrated in the section on figure drawing, pages 8–11).

2   The sketch was developed over the figure.

3   The finished sketch was shaded
    with coloured pencils, applied with
    varying degrees of pressure to
    achieve different tonal effects,
    before being cut out and mounted
    against a background. Working
    drawings were then added to
    complete the presentation.

Jogging

The figure illustrated here was developed from a photograph of a friend, taken whilst on holiday. It was stylized as a fashion sketch, using the pose as the inspiration for design ideas. Note the three stages of working. The final presentation board was produced with a watercolour wash (Reeves paintbox). A thick line was drawn around the figure with a black Pentel Sign pen. A background photograph was enlarged on a photocopier in black and white, and Spraymounted on to the board. The figure was cut out and placed against this background. Note the white edge deliberately left around the outline, to make the figure stand out against its backdrop.

Swimwear

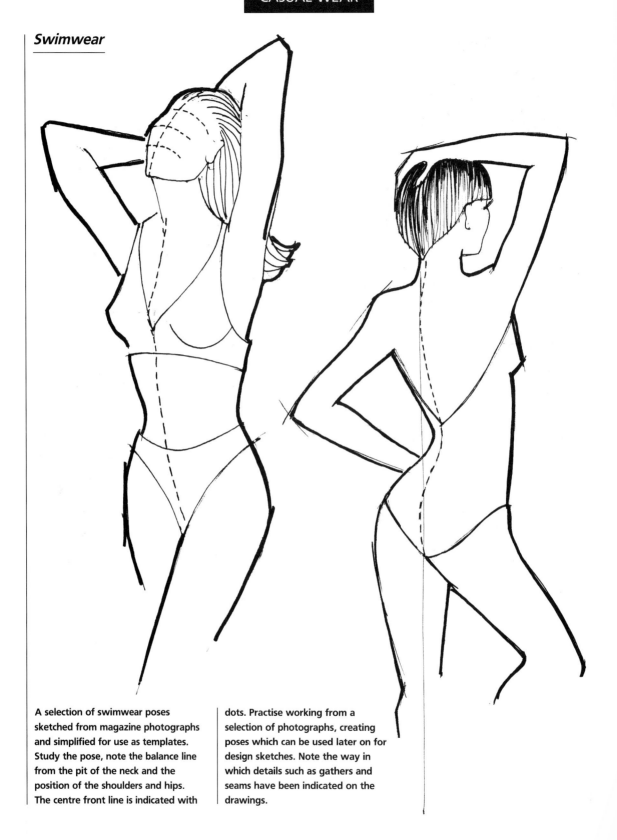

A selection of swimwear poses sketched from magazine photographs and simplified for use as templates. Study the pose, note the balance line from the pit of the neck and the position of the shoulders and hips. The centre front line is indicated with dots. Practise working from a selection of photographs, creating poses which can be used later on for design sketches. Note the way in which details such as gathers and seams have been indicated on the drawings.

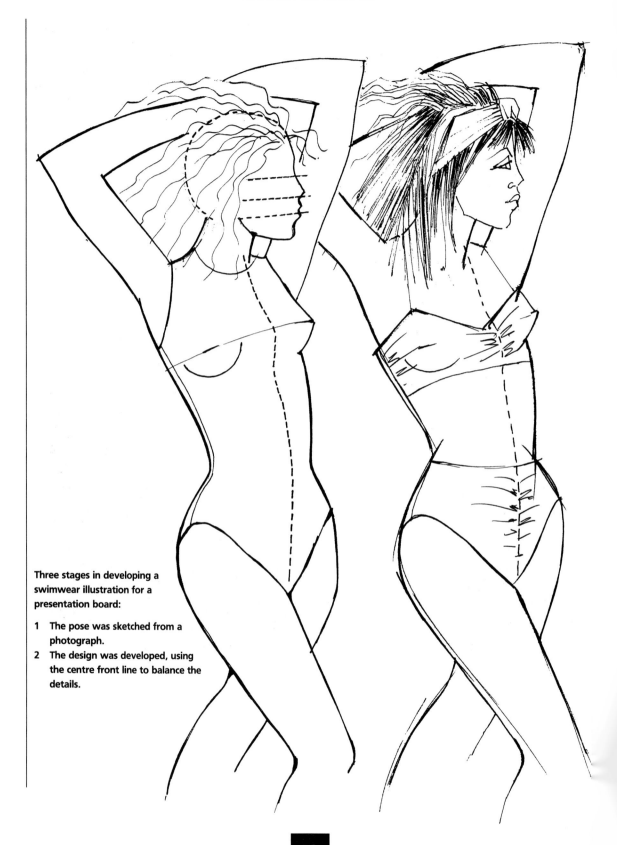

Three stages in developing a
swimwear illustration for a
presentation board:

1 The pose was sketched from a
   photograph.
2 The design was developed, using
   the centre front line to balance the
   details.

3   The final presentation. The figure
    was cut out and mounted on to a
    sheet of card. The seaside
    photograph was enlarged using a
    photocopier, and arranged on the
    board together with sample
    fabrics.

Prints

Develop patterns from actual samples of fabric and experiment with different media to achieve a variety of effects. Remember to reduce the pattern to the same scale as the figure.

This sketch was produced with a Fine Artline pen 04. A pattern was then added using a Pentel Sign pen, with areas of white left to suggest the print.

In the completed presentation drawings, the details of the pattern were added in watercolour with a fine brush, gathers and seams were then sketched in with a Fine Artline pen. A watercolour wash was added to the hair and figure.

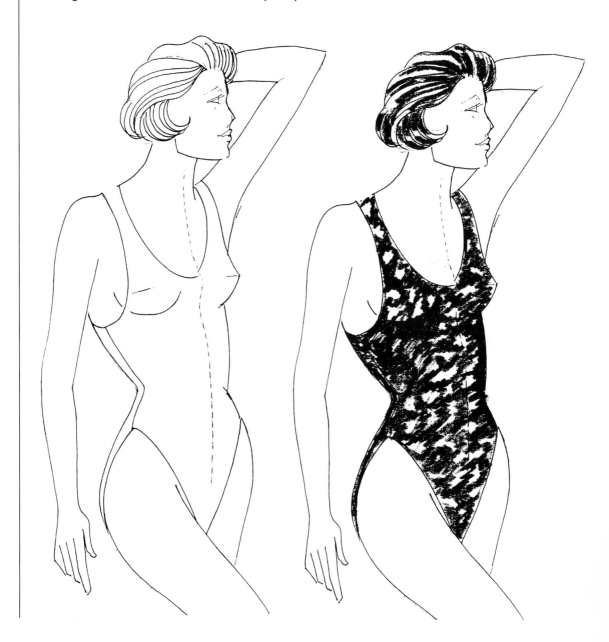

Beachwear

The design drawings illustrated here were developed in two stages:

1 The figure pose was developed from a photograph in a fashion magazine, and the outline was simplified.

2 The finished design presentation was drawn using a Fine Artline pen and completed by applying a watercolour wash to the face, arms and legs. Note the shadow applied to one side of the body to achieve the effect of light. The stripes on the trousers were painted in using a fine brush.

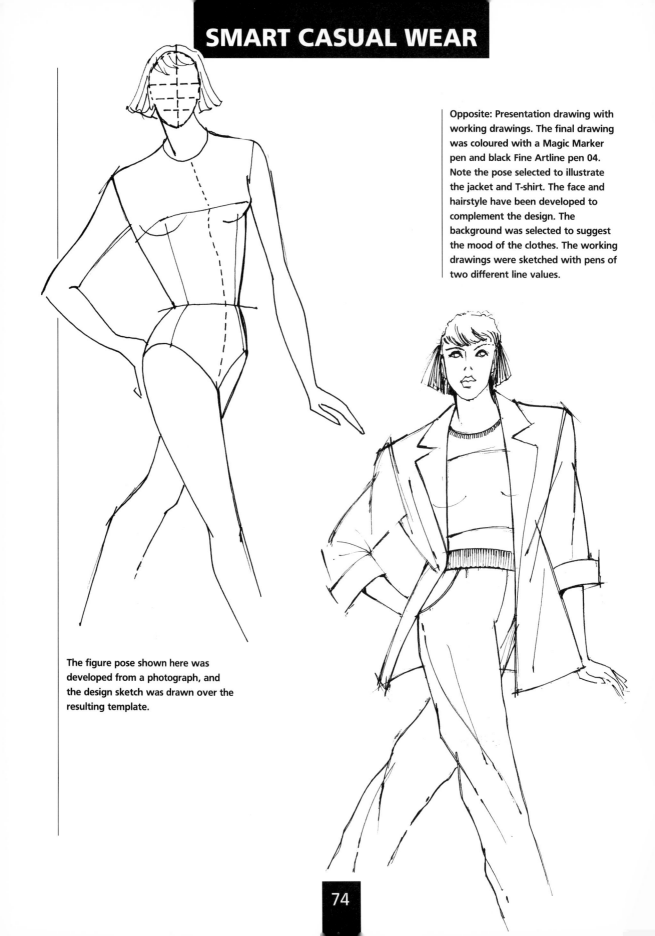

Opposite: Presentation drawing with working drawings. The final drawing was coloured with a Magic Marker pen and black Fine Artline pen 04. Note the pose selected to illustrate the jacket and T-shirt. The face and hairstyle have been developed to complement the design. The background was selected to suggest the mood of the clothes. The working drawings were sketched with pens of two different line values.

The figure pose shown here was developed from a photograph, and the design sketch was drawn over the resulting template.

The figure pose illustrated here was drawn from a model. The design drawing was developed over the figure as a line drawing, using a fine black pencil.

The jacket and skirt were shaded in with a soft grey pencil to suggest the folds in the garment. The final details were added with a fine black pen.

These sketches were produced with a Caran D'Ache Supracolor II soft pencil, using a stylized effect with emphasis on the length of the legs. Note the use of different pressures on the pencil, to give the effect of tonal contrast and pattern. Light has been suggested on the right side of the figure by using a dark tone on the left side. Experiment with a soft pencil, working from fabric samples to develop different patterns, textures and weaves.

The drawings shown here were developed from photographs. The designs were sketched over the basic template.

Note the shading which has been added to this drawing with soft black pencil, to give depth to the folds of the skirt, and to emphasize the swing of the jacket.

Skirt with accordion pleats worn with a hooded top.

Skirts and tops

Experiment with different textures and patterns. Select samples of various textures and work with several kinds of medium to achieve the effects required. When working on a design sketch, it is not necessary to illustrate the pattern or texture in great detail as shown on this page. However, when working on a fashion presentation drawing, more detail is required.

Full bias-cut circular skirt worn with a polo neck.

Skirt with box pleats worn with a V-necked top.

1 The figure pose was developed from a photograph.
2 The design was sketched over the template using a Caran D'Ache Supracolor II soft pencil. Note the free style of shading, used here to suggest the textures of the garments. The shading has been added on one side of the figure to suggest the direction of the light source. The hair, beads and details have been added in with a Fine Artline pen.

Coats and jackets

Produce one sketch, as shown here, and reproduce it several times using a photocopier or by tracing it over a light box. Apply different patterns working from a selection of fabrics, using watercolours, paints, markers or crayons. Remember that the pattern need only be suggested on the sketch, and areas should be left white to give a free impression.

The animal print effect has been achieved here by use of soft pencils.

Texture and pattern effects developed
by placing textured surfaces under
layout paper and applying a soft
pencil over the surface of the paper.

Dresses

When building up practice in reproducing patterns on design drawings, try copying a sketch several times (using a photocopier or light box) and experiment with different patterns and prints on each outline. Work from a selection of patterned fabric samples, using different media to obtain the effects required (pencils, paints or markers). Remember to reduce the patterns down to the correct scale. Fine detail is only required for presentation drawings, not for design sketches.

The pattern effect in this drawing was created using watercolours.

The original sketch in this illustration was produced using a Pilot Hi-Tecpoint V5 pen. It was photocopied several times, and different patterns were developed as described above.

These dresses were sketched from fashion models using a soft 3B pencil and a free style of drawing. Different lengths and styles of evening wear have been chosen.

These drawings were developed by working over the original drawing in two contrasting styles. In the first drawing soft pencils were used, and in the second, black pens (Pilot Hi-Tecpoint V7 Fine and Pentel Felt-tip Sign pen, which gives a thick line). A grey watercolour wash was added to suggest the gathers and folds with darker tones used to indicate the depth of the folds.

Note the beaded effect achieved here by applying white paint with a fine brush to the dark top.

A watercolour wash can be used to suggest transparency in pleated garments. Here it has been brushed over a pen-and-ink line drawing.

The importance of creating accurate working drawings (or 'flats'), for production departments cannot be overestimated. Every detail of

Casual jacket, front and back views with detailed drawing of the neck fastening. Note the balance of the pockets, sleeves and collar. The drawing was produced with three pens of different line values.

the design must be clearly shown on the working drawing, which is an analysis of the fashion sketch. All practical aspects of the design must be considered. The placement of seams, pockets, yokes and dart positions should be indicated.

The design should be shown from both front and back

views. Where a design has intricate detail, this should be drawn separately, with additional notes to explain details which may not be easily understood from the drawing.

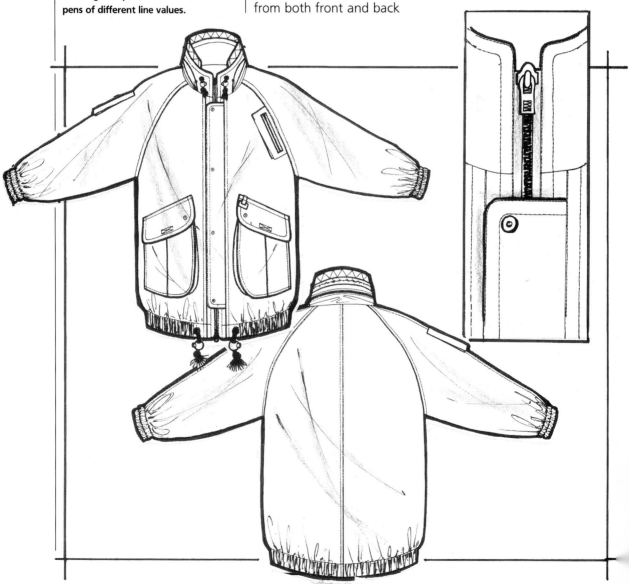

Working drawings for an evening dress, showing both front and back views.

Working drawings for short and long raincoats, with all details accurately noted.

Photocopiers

The photocopier is an invaluable tool for the fashion design illustrator. The photocopier can be used to:

1 enlarge and reduce drawings

2 reproduce drawings on which to experiment with colour, pattern and texture techniques before working on the original

3 produce material for background effects on presentation boards

4 transfer drawings onto different coloured papers

5 transfer drawings and photographs onto acetate – which is very effective for presentation work

6 paste-up drawings when working on the arrangement of design work. Cut out the figures and general artwork, and use Spraymount to fix it onto clean white card. Photocopy in black and white or colour for a clean, professional look

7 photocopy artwork for reference when sending your originals off for competitions, etc

8 photocopy reference work when researching and collecting material for sketchbooks and storyboards

9 enlarge sections of design drawings, details of collars, pockets, and style features

10 photocopy textured and patterned materials, reducing the size to match the scale of the drawing when using a collage technique, or to apply paper to the drawing

11 photocopy airbrush effects for backgrounds, then use Spraymount to attach your artwork onto it.

Marker pens

Marker pens are available in a wide range of colours and sizes, with many different nib sizes, from cylinder-shaped heads, blunt bullet-like points, wedge shapes and fine points. The inks are either water-soluble or spirit-based. Markers can be used for filling in areas of colour or for making bold outlines, to give a clean and pleasing effect. They are extremely convenient as they dry rapidly and are especially noted for their clarity of colour.

Pastels

Although no brushes are used, the use of pastels is more akin to painting than drawing – the advantage being that there is no liquid medium and hence no drying time to consider. The range of tints in each colour is considerable. A variety of tones can be achieved by treating the tinted paper as a mid-tone, and a coloured paper may be used as a key for the rest of the colour scheme. Different effects can be created, depending on which part of the pastel stick is used.

Watercolour

Watercolours may be bought as solid tablets or as paste in tubes, thinned with water before use. Paintboxes of different sizes are easily available. Paintbrushes vary in quality from sable to nylon. The paper surface is important. Unless you are using good quality paper, it should be stretched. If this is not done, the paper will react to the water by cockling, and your work will be distorted.

Gouache

Gouache is basically the same as watercolour but it is mixed with white pigment, which makes it opaque. When dry, gouache forms a positive film of colour. Hard divisions of solid colour are associated with it. A free style of painting may also be achieved where the brush strokes are visible, working with wet paint on wet paper. Watercolour paper or boards are most suitable for gouache. Cartridge and layout papers are not suitable.

Coloured pencils

A wide range of coloured pencils is available, graded from very hard to extra soft. Pencils offer the most versatile methods of colouring a drawing. By varying the pressure, different tone values may be obtained.

Water-soluble pencils are available in a wide colour range. To use them, the drawing is produced as normal, and then a watercolour wash is applied to produce an even colour, which obliterates the pencil marks.

Wax and water-solvent crayons

A large selection of wax crayons in various different thicknesses is available. A solid, bright colour can be produced, and the harder the pressure, the deeper the tone. Some crayons are wax-based, which enables you to scratch into them for surface and texture effects. Others are water-based, and may be used combined with water.

Inks

Pen and ink creates immediate visual effects, in both line and tone, which may take the form of lines, dots, hatching and cross-hatching. Ink drawings combined with washes of coloured inks are most effective. Many different colours are available. Inks can either be used on their own, mixed together, or diluted with water.

Wax-resistant effects

A wax crayon or candle may be used as a resistant to watercolour and inks. First draw with the candle to make the paper waterproof beneath the wax. Add a wash and the area will remain free of colour. A rubber solution may also be used to gain a similar effect.

Light box

A box with a glass top containing a light for tracing. By placing the work to be traced under a sheet of a paper which rests on the glass and is illuminated underneath by the light, the work is then shown clearly. These boxes are available in a range of sizes.

Airbrush

The airbrush provides perfect even tones, graded tones and soft lines. It will also blend colour. It is operated by a motor compressor or compressed air propellant aerosols.

Layout paper

White layout detail paper with a surface ideal for ink and pencil. The paper is semi-transparent, which is useful when working over roughs and developing work.

Lace evening dresses:
The effect of the lace pattern has been obtained by using a sample of lace placed under thin layout paper. The paper was then rubbed in the appropriate areas of the sketch with soft black pencil.

BOOKLIST

FASHION ILLUSTRATION

Barnes, Colin, *Fashion Illustration*, Mcdonald, 1988

Drake, Nicholas, *Fashion Illustration Today*, Thames & Hudson, 1987

Ireland, Patrick John, *Fashion Design*, Cambridge University Press, 1987

Ireland, Patrick John, *Fashion Design Drawing and Illustration*, Batsford, 1982

Ireland, Patrick John, *Encyclopedia of Fashion Details*, Batsford, 1987, 1989

Kumager, Kojiro, *Fashion Illustrations*, Graphic-Sha, 1988

Parker, William, *Fashion Drawing in Vogue*, Thames & Hudson, 1983

Yajima, Isao, *Figure Drawing for Fashion*, Graphic-Sha, 1990

Yajima, Isao, *Mode Drawing*, Graphic-Sha, 1989

FIGURE DRAWING

Croney, John, *Drawing Figure Movement*, Batsford, 1983

Everett, Felicity, *Fashion Design*, Usborne, 1987

Gordon, Louise, *Anatomy and Figure Drawing*, Batsford, 1988

Loomis, Andrew, *Figure Drawing for all it's Worth*, Viking Press, 1971

Smith, Stan and Wheeler, Linda, *Drawing and Painting the Figure*, Phaidon, 1983

GRAPHICS

Dalley, Terence (Consultant Editor), *The Complete Guide to Illustration and Design Techniques and Materials*, Phaidon, 1980

Laing, J. and Davis R.S., *Graphic Tools and Techniques*, Blandford Press, 1986

Lewis, Brian, *An Introduction to Illustration*, The Apple Press, 1987

Welling, Richard, *Drawing with Markers*, Pitman, 1974

HISTORY OF FASHION

Blum, Stella, *Designs by Erté*, Dover Publications, New York, 1976

Boucher, Francis, *A History of Costume in the West*, Thames & Hudson, 1966

Davenport, Millia, *The Book of Costume*, Crown, New York, 1976

Ewing, Elizabeth and Mackrell, Alice, *History of Twentieth Century Fashion*, Batsford, New Edition, 1992

Milbank, Caroline Reynolds, *Couture – The Great Fashion Designers*, Thames & Hudson, 1985

Murray, Maggie Pexton, *Changing Styles in Fashion*, Fairchild Publications, New York, 1989

O'Hara, Georgina, *The Encyclopaedia of Fashion*, Thames & Hudson, 1986

Peacock, John, *The Chronicle of Western Costume*, Thames & Hudson, 1991

Stegemeyer, Anne, *Who's Who in Fashion*, Fairchild, 1988

Tilke, Max, *Costume Patterns and Design*, Magna Books, 1990